101 Deer Hunting Tips

Books by Peter J. Fiduccia

Whitetail Strategies

Books by Peter J. Fiduccia and Jay Cassell

The Quotable Hunter

The Greatest Whitetail Lodges and Outfitters in North America

101 Deer Hunting Tips

Practical Advice
from a Master Hunter

Peter J. Fiduccia

The Lyons Press

Guilford, Connecticut

An imprint of The Globe Pequot Press

To my parents Joe and Lucy Fiduccia and my wife and son Kate and Cody—I love you all.

The Lyons Press in an imprint of The Globe Pequot Press.

Photos by Peter J. Fiduccia: p. x, 4, 6, 13, 14, 19, 20, 24, 25, 26, 27, 29, 38, 40, 42, 43, 44, 65, 75, 84, 85, 71, 97, 98, 100, 101, 126 128, 148
Photos by Ted Rose: p. 30, 32, 35, 46, 47, 52, 54, 56, 58, 64, 68, 70, 76, 88, 90, 96, 98, 99, 102, 104, 110, 112, 113, 117, 118, 120, 124, 30, 132, 133, 136, 138, 140, 141, 146, 147, 149, 150, 152, 153
Photos by Roman Jaskolski: p. vi, viii, 2, 8, 15, 16, 18, 22, 66, 82, 83, 123
Photo by Eastern Fishing Outdoor Expos: p. 10
Photos by Pete Rickard Scents: p. 53, 77, 78, 79, 109
Illustration on page 114 by Frank Sansavera
Photo by Richard Combs: p. 50
Photo by NorthCountry Whitetails: p. 133 (top)

Printed in the United States of America

Designed by Compset, Inc.

10 9 8 7 6 5 4 3 2 1

Library of Congress Cataloging-in-Publication Data

Fiduccia, Peter.
    101 deer hunting tips : practical advice from a master hunter /
        Peter J. Fiduccia.
      p. cm.
    ISBN 1-58574-335-6
    1. Deer hunting. I. Title: One hundred one hunting tips. II. Title.

SK301.F52 2001
799.2'765—dc21   2001050268

Contents

Foreword
by Jay Cassell

If you've never attended one of Peter Fiduccia's deer hunting seminars, you don't know what you're missing. Bantering with the audience, conversing with people in a give-and-take style, asking questions, and at the end of the lecture, rewarding correct answers with his book, a bottle of scent, or perhaps his rattling or deer calling video, Fiduccia knows how to keep an audience's attention! They love him!

Fact is, they love him, but they also completely relate to his message—which is, in essence, that hunters have to pay attention to the smallest detail, to create illusions to fool or attract deer. What are the illusions? That you're a competitive buck looking for a fight. That you're a doe in heat, waiting for a buck to pay attention to her. That you're really not there at all—what the buck smells is apple scent—not a human.

Demonstrating with deer calls, rattling antlers, deer tails, fake apples and more, Fiduccia leads his audience along the deer hunter's trail, teaching the various tactics and strategies that have taken him more than 30 deer seasons to learn. By the end of the seminar, you applaud him roundly, for he has not only shared his best-kept deer hunting secrets with you, but has gotten you totally pumped to go hunting—right now!

I've known Peter for 20 years now. I've hunted with him many times. I've heard other people sing his praises. But more important, I've seen him in action in the deer woods—how he moves, how he notices the smallest of sign, how he figures things out. Once, when I received permission to hunt a new piece of property, Peter pulled out a map and, without ever even stepping foot on the land, showed me exactly where the mature bucks would bed and travel—"Here, on this knoll, and this trail here, leading to the swamp, that is definitely a funnel that they regularly use. You should set up here, and here." And, of course, he was right. I placed another hunter in a stand in the spot Peter marked on the map and, sure enough, he took a nice buck on his first day there.

Peter is a business associate as well as my friend. We talk all the time. And every year it's the same story—he's working, he wishes he had more time to get out and hunt, he couldn't get out this morning. But you know what? No matter the complications, no matter what part of New York he hunts, he gets a big buck every year. He figures it out, then goes afield—often midday—when he feels all the elements are right, and gets the job done. It's amazing. He practices what he preaches and it works!

I've also seen him do it on the road, hunting in new country in a different state. I've seen him tell guides that the tactics they are using are wrong, that they should be hunting here, not there. And they'll object, but Peter will insist on putting his stand where he wants. And guess what? He'll take a nice buck soon after making the change.

What you are about to read is a compilation of 101 of Peter's favorite deer hunting tips. They aren't all of his tactics, but there are a lot of his best ones. But the fact is, it would be hard to put all of his strategies to paper, no matter what. For a lot of what of what Peter does in the deer woods is based on common sense and observation. He reads sign that's happening in the woods—where the rubs are, how many scrapes, the temperature, wind direction, moon phase, rain or snow—and puts it all together in that deer-hunting computer sitting on top of his neck to formulate a working strategy—every time he's afield. Then he goes forth and gets his buck.

Preface

This book is meant to make your deer hunting more successful and more enjoyable. It is small enough to be kept in a daypack for reference, a cupboard in hunting camp (to generate fuel other than for heating), or in the glove compartment of your truck. Of course, a place on your library wouldn't hurt my feelings either.

I have included my deer hunting tips that have worked for me consistently over my 35 years of hunting whitetails. Both the sage and the novice will find these tips new and useful. The tactic tips are meant to help you score on a good buck the very next time you go deer hunting. The general tips are solid information to help round out your deer hunting savvy.

When reading this book, remember that when it comes to hunting whitetails, being creative and using strategies that are out-of-the-box will produce results. Break out of the mold. Don't hunt the same way in the same areas day after day, year after year. It's hard to do, but make a pact with yourself to try different things at different times of the day. You won't regret it, just these simple things will put a good buck in your sights this season!

Most of all, be confident in your hunting ability. Trust your deer hunting judgement. Each time you go afield, tell yourself—I'm a good hunter, my tactics are sound and what ever decision I make about where to take a stand or if I should call, rattle or just sit patiently is the strategy that will work today. I know I'm going to see a buck. Remember, confidence is the name of the game in deer hunting as in life. The more confidence you have, the more success will follow.

Good hunting,
Peter Fiduccia
The Deer Doctor

Acknowledgments

I want to thank Tony Lyons for his ongoing support. He is a friend's friend. Someone a person can trust and count on through thick and thin. I can only hope my friendship means as much to him as his does to me. I would also like to thank my longtime buddy and associate Jay Cassell for his expertise with editing this book. Jay and I have hunted and worked together for 20 years—I look forward to 20 more years of sharing hunting and fishing adventures with him. Of course, I want to extend my warmest appreciation to you—my readers and viewers. Without your dedicated support over the past 20 years, I would still be working as a general manager in the hotel and restaurant business in Vail, Colorado!

PART 1

Getting Permission

Obtaining permission to hunt posted lands can be the key to successful hunting. It's not as difficult as most hunters think, either. It just takes patience, persistence, and a lot of common sense.

1 The earlier you start knocking on doors of farmers' homes, the better. When I'm planning to approach farmers and ask them for permission to hunt, I usually start in December or January, after the holidays are over. This is generally a downtime for them. Asking farmers in summer and fall almost guarantees receiving a no. Farmers like to talk and make friends like anyone else, but *only* when they're not busy with planting, feeding, harvesting, and repairing equipment.

2 Never, *ever* knock on the door of someone you are looking to get permission from dressed in your hunting clothes. I have received many more positive responses by approaching people dressed in clean, neat street clothes.

3 Always show up with a sample Hold Harmless release (an informal agreement releasing the landowner from any responsibility should you be injured while hunting on his property). It will help make the job of getting a yes much easier.

4 Let landowners know that you will treat the land as if it were your own. Tell them you will leave gates and fences as you found them, that you will remove any litter you see and not leave any of your own, and that you will post the property if they want you to.

5 Lastly, let them know how appreciative you would be to hunt their lands. Explain that you would be happy to share any game. Treat them to a special dinner at a fine restaurant once or twice a year, or ask what type of wine they like to drink and send them a few bottles. You could also let them know you would be happy to pay a small fee for the privilege to hunt the land. You'll be surprised to find out that most will decline all of the above, but feel a lot better about you—and perhaps good enough to allow you to hunt their lands.

PART 2

Booking an Outfitter

If you want to hunt a new area, outside your home state, a viable option is to book an outfitter. To make sure the lodge or outfitter you select is reliable, and will provide you with the best opportunity to bag a buck of your dreams, keep these suggestions in mind.

6 If you book your hunt at a sportsman's show, go to the out-fitter's booth you're thinking of booking, but don't approach it until he is talking with someone else. Then nonchalantly stand around, close to the booth but not right at it. Look and listen to what he says and does with other hunters he is talking to—as you glance through his brochure. I usually do this at least two times. I want to find out if the intended outfitter is an even-tempered person. I want to hear if he tells everyone the same *exact* thing. I notice if he answers all the questions asked of him—eagerly. If he doesn't pass this first test with flying colors, he's probably not an outfitter I want to hunt with. If he is short-tempered at the show, imagine how he'll be at his lodge after he has your money!

7 Talk to him as a businessperson, not as his pal. Gain his respect right from the start by asking intelligent questions about the hunt and the facilities. Most important, take notes at the booth. That will set the tone from the get-go that you're not the average hunter. He'll also know that the information he gives you at the booth will have to match what happens at the hunt. He'll be more straightforward with you. If he complains, or makes any curt or rude comment about the note taking—move on!

8 Ask questions about the hunt first. How long have his guides been with him? What type of hunting tactics does he use? What type of terrain will you be hunting? How long is the average shot? What caliber and loads does he suggest? Is there a lot of walking to be done? Do they drive deer? Mention that you do not want to hunt from a vehicle, as some outfitters use the truck as a blind. Ask if they hunt all day or just in the morning and evening. Explain what type of hunting you like to do (rattling, calling, still-hunting, posting, etc.), and ask if they either participate in such tactics or even allow them.

9 Find out if the outfitter charges a trophy fee, and, if so, how much. Ask if there are any hidden costs, and if they will field-dress, cape, and skin your deer. Find out if the outfitter has a walk-in cooler on site, and if there are facilities close by that butcher, wrap, label, and ship the meat back home. Talk to him about the tipping policy: What do his guides "expect" as an average gratuity? Find out what the sleeping arrangements are: Do you share a room or bunk with someone? If so, and you're a non-smoker, let him know you don't want to be around someone who does smoke. Find out how the camp or lodge is heated: This may sound like a no-brainer, but I can't tell you how many times I have been cold in camps that turn off the generator at night. Don't be shy about asking if there are hot showers, and if you can shower at least once a day. Ask what type of food they serve and if they will they cater to special diets. Find out how many hunters the outfitter takes in per week. Does he allow cigarette smoking in the lodge and at dinner? Are there facilities to wash and dry clothes and footwear? Does he have a phone and can you make outgoing calls on it? How close is the nearest hospital or medical facility?

10 Ask what type of stands he uses: wood or metal shooting houses? Heated or unheated? Are the treestands permanent structures or portable ones? Are you left in a stand by yourself? If so (and this is especially important when hunting in cold weather places like Manitoba, Alberta, and Saskatchewan), for what periods of time? For instance, some ranches do not allow hunters to leave their stands to still-hunt, while others will allow a hunter to stalk as long as he's accompanied by a guide. Others put hunters in comfortable shooting houses for three to five hours in the morning, bring them back to the lodge for lunch, and take them out again for a few hours of hunting in the evening. Whichever type of blind you're in, make sure they know how long you like to stay out.

11 The key to having an enjoyable hunt is not only to check out the references of successful hunters that the guide supplies you. They are bound to give the kinds of endorsements he wants you to hear. The key is to ask the references about how hunters who didn't score felt. Did they blame the guide for not doing his job or just attribute not taking a deer to "the way it goes"? Call the owner/manager of the lodge back a few times and talk about the hunt again. Keep asking questions. If they lose patience with you, then this isn't a place to book. Don't be shy. These hunts aren't cheap, and you work hard for your money. You deserve to get what you pay for. Most outfitters—a majority of them—are reliable and want to do all they can to make your hunt a success. They'll be more than happy to answer your inquiries.

12 Most outfitters have their own Web sites, so pay their sites a visit, and read through them carefully. Also ask the outfitter if he has a promotional video that you can look at. It will clearly document the ranch, its facilities, the happy clients, and, most important, the class of bucks that they take there.

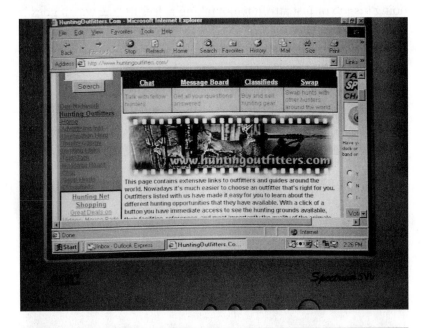

13 The most important advice I can give you about booking a hunt is the things not to do or say. When speaking with the outfitter, especially at a sportsman's show, *don't* whip out your success photos or bore him to death with your stories. This is not the time or place to do that. He is there to book hunts and needs to talk to as many potential clients as possible. *Don't* talk about the size of the buck you won't shoot; he hears that from almost every hunter and has learned that most hunters will shoot the first decent buck that comes along. *Don't* talk about other outfitters—good or bad. *Don't* make suggestions about how he can improve his bookings. *Don't* tell him you're going to bring him a lot of business. *Don't* try to negotiate a lower price—you'll get what you pay for. Finally, *don't* brag about your deer hunting prowess.

14 Despite your best efforts, keep in mind that hunting is hunting. No matter where or whom you hunt with, there are times when things just don't go right. Mother Nature has her own plans. An outfitter can't do a thing about the weather or unforeseen emergencies. If he tries hard to get you an animal and it doesn't work out—and all the other elements of the hunt were good—you'll have to give him another opportunity to judge him fairly.

15

PART 3

Traveling with Firearms and Bows

To prevent last-minute problems when traveling by air with firearms, a hunter must be familiar with the airline guidelines regarding firearms and ammunition. Not knowing what the airlines require can create nightmares at check-in, causing delays or even a missed flight. Being prepared and knowing the regulations will make airline travel snag-free. In today's world of heightened airline security, following ALL the rules and allowing extra time for inspection of firearm baggage is not only wise, it's practical. Following are some tips that generally apply to all airlines.

15 Before departing for the terminal, call the airline and ask about its firearms restrictions. Over the years, I have had agents from the same airline give me different information. A better and safer way to get the airline's firearm restrictions is to get them online, or request that they be faxed to you. Go to the airline's Web site, find their firearms regulations, and print them out. By doing that, once you get to the counter, you won't risk an agent contradicting what another agent may have told you. You'll have the restrictions in your hand—directly from the airline's own Web site.

16 Remember to allow for the appropriate amount of time to check your luggage and firearms at the counter. Ticket agents will require you to demonstrate in an isolated area that the firearm is unloaded. You'll then be asked to sign a form stating the firearm is "Unloaded," which will then be placed into the locked gun case. At that time, they will also hand you a form to sign called a Firearm Declaration Tag.

17 Almost all airlines require that the gun be in a hard-sided, locking case. The case must be locked and the key or combination must remain in your possession.

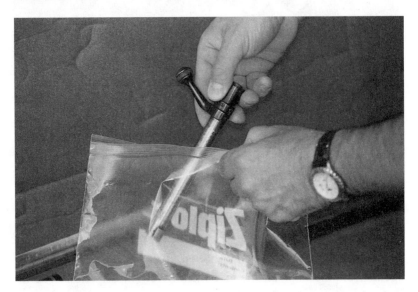

18 When traveling with a bolt-action rifle, remove the bolt from the firearm, put it in a small plastic bag, and pack it inside the gun case with the rifle. Don't leave it in the firearm. When possible, remove or leave open all actions of firearms inside their case. This will make it easier for an airline official to ascertain that your firearm, indeed, is not loaded.

19 Although some airlines allow ammunition to be packed with the firearm, other airlines do not. If your flight is delayed or canceled and you are transferred to another airline that doesn't allow ammunition to be packed with a firearm, you'll be asked to remove it. To avoid complications, I always pack ammunition in another case. You'll be asked to identify what baggage it is in, so the agent can mark that luggage with the appropriate "Live Ammunition" sticker. Most airlines will not allow customers to take more than 11 pounds of ammunition.

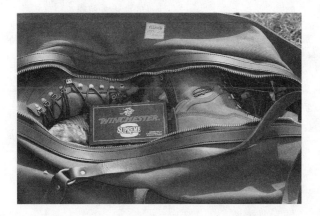

20 Archers will have generally the same guidelines for packing. The hard locking case can include one bow, one quiver with arrows and broadheads, and a maintenance kit.

PART 4

Sighting In

The process of zeroing-in a firearm involves making the firearm and the sight coincide on the exact spot where the bullet will hit. When done correctly, sighting in a firearm isn't difficult. In fact, it can be quick, easy, and a lot of fun.

21 The first element to accurate shooting is to make sure that each and every screw is tightened securely on both the firearm and the scope mounts. This is especially true for the screws that hold the stock to the barrel. When these screws are not secure, it will cause the rifle to shoot inaccurately.

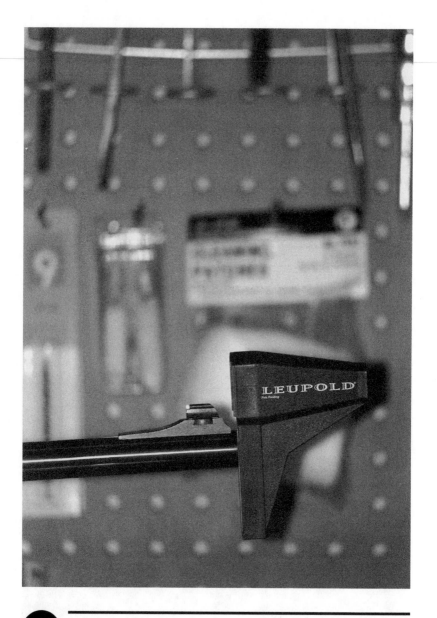

22 Contrary to popular belief, bore sighting or using a collimator is not a substitute for actually sighting in a firearm at the range. Bore sighting is only meant to get a firearm 'on the paper' at a distance that's usually 100 yards. This means a gun that is bore sighted could have a bullet that shoots high, low, left, or right of the bull's-eye by several inches.

23 Always sight in a rifle with the same brand and bullet weights. Almost all firearms will shoot particular brands, types, and weights of ammunitions differently, each changing the rifle's point-of-impact and thus requiring another round of sighting in. The fact is that each rifle barrel will "favor" a certain load and type of shell over another. For instance, I have a .280-caliber bolt action that drives tacks when I shoot 140-grain pointed soft-point Core-Lok cartridges out of it. When I shoot any other type of .280 ammo, the rifle shoots less accurate groupings. Sight in with the particular brand, type, and weight of ammo that you intend to use in the field for maximum accuracy.

24 When shooting at the range, you may find that your bullets are beginning to "walk" all over the target, causing you trouble in grouping your shots. This may be due to a hot barrel. Many firearms will begin to shoot ammunition erratically when the barrel gets too hot. When this happens, let the barrel cool down totally before you resume shooting.

25 For best results, always sight in from a solid rest, such as a sand bag or bench rest. A solid anchor point will improve your accuracy tremendously at the range and in the field. Begin at 25 yards, and carefully squeeze off three aimed shots. The center of this group of bullet holes is the rifle's POI (point of impact). Adjusting the sight or scope moves the POI to the desired zero or mark. Move open rear sights in the same direction you want the group to move. Adjust scopes by following the directions (usually arrows) on the dials. Do not adjust sights based on the results of one shot. An errant shot can lead to sight-adjustment errors and a lot of wasted ammo and frustration. Once you have determined that the firearm is on paper at 25 yards, place a new target at whatever distance you want to shoot in the field and verify the rifle's zero at that distance.

26 Your firearm may have been dropped or bumped around while in transit—in a car or plane, on a horse, and so on. As a precaution, take the time to confirm that the zero hasn't moved before you begin your hunt. This single practice could make the difference in bagging your trophy or missing it.

PART 5

Camp Protocol

As a guest at someone else's deer camp, there are protocols that you should follow—if you want to get a return invitation, that is.

27 Never ask what you can do; instead, ask what your *assigned* chores are during your stay. And don't take "don't worry about chores, you're our guest" for an answer. Let the host know you want to be part of the group and that you are more comfortable pitching in. Start by asking if there are any areas of the property that need fresh posters.

28 Help out during the hunt as well. Help fellow hunters field-dress and drag their deer back to camp. Help hang the deer. Offer to take photos of the successful hunter and his trophy. During dinner, make sure you give a sincere congratulations to everyone who has bagged a buck that day.

29 Don't be afraid to volunteer to be a driver during pushes, even if you don't know the lay of the land. Tell the host that driving is a way for you to learn the property in the event you're ever invited back. If it's really a complicated piece of ground to drive, ask to be assigned a route that isn't as likely to get you lost, rather than make an excuse not to drive. No one likes a hunter who wants to take a stand every time a drive is made.

30 If a deer is wounded, volunteer to help look for it, even if it's cold, rainy, or at night. Be enthused about the search and give 110 percent to help locate another hunter's wounded deer.

31 When placed on a stand and told to "stay here until we pick you up"—do just that. Don't move off the stand and start walking around. This can be one of the quickest ways not to get invited back. If you can't post for a long time, tell your hosts that when they invite you—not after they get angry that you have left your stand and caused a problem for another hunter nearby.

32 Make sure you arrive with your firearm or bow sighted in. Taking a lot of shots to sight in a rifle at camp is not appropriate for a guest. You could be taking sighting-in time away from the host and members of his family. Arriving with a sighted-in firearm also speaks highly of your woodsmanship.

33 Don't arrive empty-handed. Bring some type of cooked food. Putting a big pan of lasagna, or some steaks, or a couple of dozen chicken cutlets, or several pies and other desserts in the refrigerator when you walk in will help to break the ice.

34 Here's my pet peeve. I absolutely never invite back anyone who shoots a deer and then comes up with a reason to leave camp. If you have been invited for a week or a weekend and you shoot a buck early, plan to stay for the entire time anyway. You can act as a driver, or help around the cabin, or cut wood for next season. Remember, you weren't invited to shoot and leave. You were asked to come to be part of the camaraderie.

PART 6

Dress to Kill

*To remain on stand longer, or to have even half
a chance at staying in the woods all day, a hunter
must be dressed for the weather conditions at hand.
In fact, dressing correctly is one of the most
overlooked tactics by hunters. Simply, if you're
freezing cold, or wet, or overheated on a hot day,
you are not going to hunt effectively. When I go deer
hunting, I don't worry about fashion. But I do dress
to kill. You should too, for the longer you remain on
your stand, or in the woods, the greater your
chances of seeing more deer or taking a buck.*

35 Ninety percent of body heat is lost through the head. By covering your head with a nylon stocking and then a wool cap, you'll dramatically reduce the loss of body heat from your head. Covering your neck with a turtleneck and a scarf will also keep you much warmer, as will protecting your ears. During extremely cold conditions, use a wool pullover face mask in conjunction with the above items, and you'll be able to remain on stand for long periods of time without getting cold.

36 Keeping your hands warm is also an important element to staying in the woods for longer periods of time. Cold fingers will not only make you miserable, but can seriously interfere with your ability to shoot properly. Many a hunter has lost the opportunity to shoot a buck because his hands and fingers were too cold to work the action or reload another shell or even squeeze off a shot without shaking. To keep your hands the warmest, wear insulated mittens. You can pull a mitten off in plenty of time when you see an approaching buck. Other options include mittens with shooting fingers and thick gloves with all the fingers (although these latter gloves will not keep your hands as warm as the mitten types).

37 Cold feet will end any hunt prematurely, for once your feet become cold, getting them warm without leaving your stand and walking around is hard to do. If there is any area where you should buy the best you can afford, it's footwear. Buy a good pair of boots, with 1,000 or more grams of insulation, wear them with one pair of socks, and your feet should stay toasty even on frigid days.

38 Today's high-tech leather boots are 100 percent waterproof, and they breathe too—thus allowing moisture to evaporate and keeping your feet dry. If you are going to be standing in or walking through water for long periods during the hunt, however, it's better to wear rubber boots with thick socks.

39 Another way to stay warm on stand for longer periods of time is to give your body some extra fuel to burn. Eat a good breakfast before going hunting. About 80 percent of the food we eat is converted into heat. To keep heat-producing levels up, you need more carbohydrates and fat and less protein. Candy, fruits, and cereals are high in carbohydrates, while butter, nuts, and chocolate are high in fat. Eat a bowl of cereal or farina, a buttered roll, and some fruit before going out, and take some candy with you to snack on. You'll stay warmer because of this. And remember that the colder the day, the more body fuel you'll burn.

PART 7

Best Times to Hunt

For as long as I can remember, I've been told that the best times to hunt deer are at dawn and dusk. While this is a peak time of deer movement and accounts for a lot of deer being seen and taken, I have found after 34 years of hunting whitetails that it isn't the necessarily the "best" time to be afield.

40 Trying to stay on stand all day isn't as good an idea as you might think. If you become cold, for example, the chances of you moving and becoming fidgety are much greater. Deer may see the movement and steer away from the area. Becoming bored after spending hours on stand also contributes to the hunter not only moving more, but not concentrating on the hunt the entire time. It only takes a big buck a few seconds to slip by a hunter who is not paying full attention to his surroundings because he has become tired or lost his concentration.

41 One strategy is to get to your stand around 8:00 a.m., no earlier. Settle in and get focused on the job at hand, for it's around this time when hunters who have already been on stand two to three hours begin to get cold or bored and begin to move from location to location. Many will start heading back to camp for breakfast or coffee by 9:00 a.m., rousting deer as they move and pushing them by a hunter who is settled in his stand and is warm, comfortable, and zeroed in on his surroundings, watching for deer.

42 Another time-of-day tactic is to move from the 8:00 a.m. location and find a fresh stand several hundred yards away. This serves two purposes. If it is an exceptionally cold morning, walking (actually still-hunting) to a new site to post will get you warm again. And once you settle in, get ready! One of the most productive times to be afield is what I like to refer to as the "off-hour" movement pattern from 11:30 a.m. to around 1:30 p.m. Deer, especially mature bucks, like to get up from their beds and move about to stretch, feed, or, during the rut, look for does—which also like to move around during this time period. I have taken some of my largest bucks between these hours.

43 After hunting the off-hour period, consider going back to the cabin or vehicle for a quick lunch or coffee break. Plan to get back in your stand no later than 2:30 p.m. Traditionally, hunters begin to return to their stands around 3:00 p.m., to settle in for the afternoon wait. Many times, they push deer past other hunters who are already in their stands. In states where turkey and deer seasons coincide, a gobbler can be a bonus, as below.

PART 8

Stalking

Stalking up on whitetails can be extremely effective, but it is difficult to do under most conditions. No matter how experienced you are, the fact is that it's tough trying to sneak up on a wily old buck when the leaves are so dry that each step sounds like you're crunching cornflakes. Still-hunting works better in some parts of the country than in others, however. In Texas, for example, there are few leaves and lots of soft sand and dirt, thus making stalking easier to do. Stalking also works better along ledges, in conifer forests, in high grassy fields, on wet ground, in soft snow, and in wind. You can also employ it when leaves are crunchy, but as a spooking tactic to push deer to hunting companions waiting on escape routes.

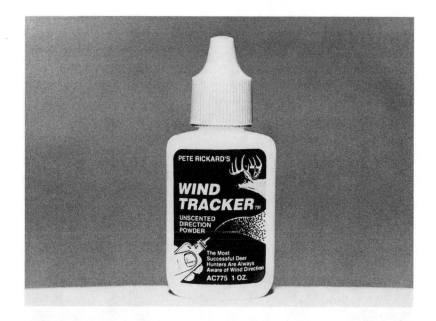

44 To become a consistently successful deer stalker, check the wind direction every few minutes. You can do this with a piece of thread tied to your gun or bow. But while the thread will show you how the wind is blowing where you're standing, it won't show you what it's doing 20 feet away. To be certain what the thermal currents are doing with your scent as you stalk ahead, especially on days without a noticeable breeze, use a commercially made wind-tracking powder. By simply squeezing out a little powder every few minutes, you'll be able to avoid having an undetectable thermal or convection current play havoc with your scent while you're still-hunting. These powders are especially useful when the wind is calm, when the thread is hanging limp. Spray some tracking powder, and chances are the powder will drift away on a current you otherwise wouldn't have noticed.

45 When still-hunting in terrain that offers distant views, such as cut corn, alfalfa, soybeans, or anywhere you can see a deer get up from a long way off, there is no real need to spend a lot of time standing and watching as you stalk. In these situations, stop and scan carefully ahead for only a few minutes, then slowly move another 30 yards. This practice will let you cover much more ground, while still allowing you to employ a poke-and-stalk type of tactic.

46 As most seasoned still-hunters know, when hunting in thick cover where you can't see far and where deer can hide in or behind every rock, blowdown, brushpile, or patch of high grass, the best tactic is to move very, very slowly. Take just a few steps, stop, look, and listen. Before moving again, stay and look a little longer.

Then check the wind and move a few more yards. Repeat the same thing over and over again as you cover the area you want to still-hunt. To move just 100 yards should take you the better part of an hour. This type of still-hunting works well in wooded areas, swamps, thickets, conifer forests, and anywhere you don't have a long, unobstructed view. Many times deer will try to hold tight as a hunter passes by. But by moving very slowly, you'll make even the cagiest buck extremely nervous. That buck may decide to get up and bolt, so always be ready to take a quick shot.

47 Once, while hunting in Texas, I tried stalking up on a known feeding area with a good view. The ground was damp and I was walking on soft sand, which made my footsteps even more quiet than usual. As I approached, I kept to the edges of the trail, keeping myself in cover and the wind in my favor. Despite my precautions, I was shocked to see a mature buck pick his head up from feeding, glance in my direction, and bolt off before I could react. With the wind blowing in my face, there was no doubt in my mind that he heard me coming.

The reason for this anecdote is to emphasize what I said earlier—that still-hunting is not easy. Unless you do it with patience, you will only end up seeing tails as deer run off for cover. And that's my best tip about still-hunting. To be a consistently successful still-hunter, you have to be *extremely* patient. Otherwise, you won't succeed.

PART 9

Drives

Taking deer by using this tactic began with our earliest hunters and ancestors—the cavemen. It is a reliable strategy that will put deer meat in the freezer when all else fails. Don't think this is a lock, however. While deer drives may work most of the time, they aren't as easy to employ as some hunters might think. Driving deer to where you would like them to go takes detailed planning, a keen understanding of the terrain, an intimate knowledge of the game, and close communication between the hunters involved. Deer have a keen knack for going where they want to go on a drive despite all of the above. Over the years I have learned that sometimes small, spur-of-the-moment drives (with one to three people) work better than an organized large drive.

48 One of my favorite small-drive tactics requires two hunters. I call it the decoy and drop drive. The best time to run it is between 9:00 a.m. and 1:00 p.m.; its main purpose is to ambush bedded bucks. The two-man drive works in all types of terrain, and is

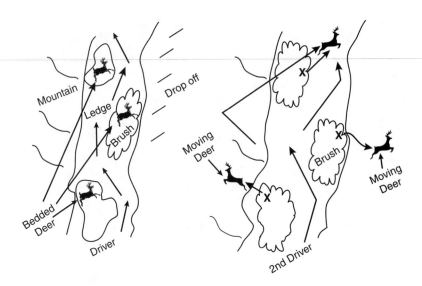

especially productive along ledges where hunters can cover as much or as little ground as they want. It also works in large standing patches of corn, thick swamps, and in heavy evergreen forests.

The first hunter begins the drive by walking with the wind in his face, parallel to the ledges, not taking advantage of cover. He wants the deer to see or hear him, but doesn't want to alarm them into breaking out ahead of him too soon. In fact, by moving slowly and stopping, he encourages the deer to try to escape once he has passed.

The second hunter waits half an hour before beginning his drive—along the same route taken by the first hunter. The key to this drive is that the first driver must walk slowly through the area, stopping often. Each time he begins to walk again, he should snap a small branch from a tree or make some other noise.

What happens is that most bucks remain bedded until the first driver has gone by. Most times, because of the slow pace of the drive, bucks become nervous and don't want to stay where they are. They get up and head back toward the direction where the first driver came from—or else head up or down the mountain, perpendicular to the first driver's path. In either case, they will eventually come into view of the second driver, who will have the shot.

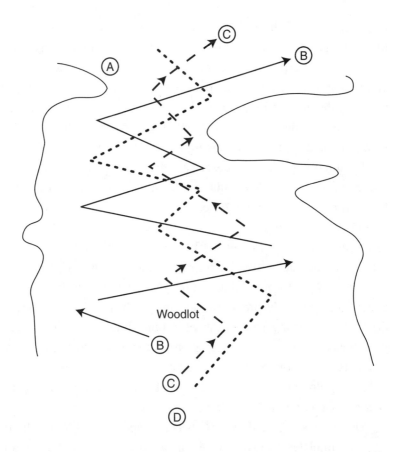

49 An offshoot of the two-man drive discussed in Tip No. 48 is the three- or four-man decoy drive. Knowing the terrain is critical to this drive's success. For example, I have found this to work best in large woodlots where I am familiar with known escape routes, bedding areas, and breakout points from the cover to open ground, which leads to other cover.

The drive begins with Driver A taking a stand ahead of the single driver who will be initiating the drive. Driver A is the point man, and must be on stand a good half hour prior to the drive's beginning. Driver B begins the drive by walking slowly through the woodlot in a wide, zig-zagging fashion. Although he could certainly get a shot at a deer, he is primarily the decoy. Again, Driver B stops often to look and even sit for several minutes. Once Driver B has gone for about 20 minutes, he is followed by Driver C, who walks behind him but zigzags in only half or one-quarter the width of Driver B's zigzagging pattern. Driver C must walk very slowly and takes advantage of as much cover as possible. When Driver B anticipates reaching the end of the woodlot, he patterns his movements to end up on the opposite end of the woods from Driver A. Then he takes up a stand and waits for deer being moved to him by Driver C.

Unlike the first drive I described, the deer on this drive usually move out quicker. At least, that has been the experience of most of the drivers who take up the A position.

Driver A's deer are usually moving at a fast walk and, in some instances, a trot. This could be because Driver B's scent is more prevalent since he is zigzagging rather than walking with his face against the wind throughout the entire drive. Traditionally, deer that wind danger quickly break out and move ahead of the oncoming driver before trying to sneak back around him. Driver C usually gets shots at deer concentrating on one of the other drivers. Driver C also gets a good opportunity when he takes up his stand at the end of the woodlot, between A and B—all of whom are now waiting for deer being moved out by Driver D.

Driver D is an added twist to this drive and acts as the fourth driver. He stimulates deer (that have outwaited and outwitted Drivers B and C), through their own sheer nervousness, to finally make a move. Driver D moves forward at a very slow rate (as if still-hunting). He takes three or four steps, stops, and waits a good five minutes before proceeding. He repeats this tactic throughout his entire drive. Optimally, Driver D is still driving long after Drivers A, B, and C have taken up their stands at the end of the woodlot. Driver D's success comes from spotting deer the other drivers did not see sneaking ahead of behind, or between them. Often, these deer are trying to get back to bedding areas that they were jumped from.

PART 10

Bad Weather

How many times have you heard that deer don't move in foul weather—in heavy wind, rain, or snow? Many studies have been done on deer movement related to wind speed and other foul-weather conditions, with many contradictory theories the result. I have taken some to heart, and some I have dismissed entirely. What I have found about hunting deer in wind, rain, or snow is that nothing about deer movement and foul weather is written in stone. But I do know this: A bad-weather day afield beats a comfortable day of sitting by a fireplace at home. Anything can happen during a hunt, bad weather or not. And nothing is going to happen if you're sitting in a chair, watching television in your living room.

50 One of the best times to hunt whitetails is during a steady downpour. Even though old-timers may say that deer bed down during heavy rain, I have found the opposite to be true. In fact, I have seen them travel as usual during rain, and sometimes even more. I have taken many mature racked bucks in rain that was coming down so hard that I had a tough time seeing them without using my scope.

51 Another good time to be afield is on days when the wind is blowing 20 to 30 mph. Although most deer seek shelter during high winds, some will keep moving until the gusts exceed 30 mph. When winds get that strong, deer become nervous and spooky, jumping at every little noise and movement. But heavy wind also covers any noises you may make as you walk to your stand, or while you're stalking. It helps to dissipate your scent quickly, too.

Once winds reach 20 mph or so, look for deer to take cover on protected lee slopes and hills and in dense conifer woodlands. Evergreens can cut wind speeds by 70 to 80 percent, so make a point of stalking hemlock and cedar groves and other conifer clusters on windy days.

52 I like to hunt on days when the wind is blowing so hard branches are breaking and trees are swaying. During these types of windy conditions deer, and especially old bucks, tend to bed down tight until the wind lightens up. They will often bed in semi-open areas such as overgrown fields, high grass, rocky out-croppings, standing cornfields, and other spots where they have a good view of their surroundings. They abandon the typical thick cover in extremely windy conditions because they can't depend on their sense of hearing to warn them of impending danger. In this type of wind I have snuck up on bucks under ledges, blowdowns in the middle of fields, and even on the sides of treeless slopes. I took most of them without the bucks ever suspecting I was there.

53 Just before and after a heavy snowstorm can be a promising time to hunt big bucks. Although it's fairly common knowledge that mature bucks will move to feed just prior to or just after a snowstorm, there is another crucial element to this puzzle: namely, that they usually move off-hours, often going to feed between 9:00 and 11:00 a.m. and then again between noon and 2:00 p.m. Being afield just before or after a big snowstorm during those times of the day can pay off.

PART 11

Moon Phases

American Indians knew about hunting with the moon. In fact, they're the ones who originated terms such as "harvest moon," "hunter's moon," and "Rutting Moon." Their very survival was dependent on knowing the best times to hunt. They quickly learned to master moon phases. Since then, there has been a lot written and said about hunting whitetails by the moon. While I'm not a total convert to lunar hunting, I have always taken moon phase into consideration when hunting any big game. It does affect game movement and behavior, and it will make a difference in your hunting. Just don't become obsessed with hunting by the moon to the degree of staying home if the moon phase isn't right.

54 During the early-fall archery season, darkness comes around 6:30 p.m. or so. Hunters will often see deer enter fields in good light (between 5:00 and 6:00 p.m.), and begin to feed. As the season wears on and dusk comes earlier each day, deer begin to feed later and later. Soon, deer are no longer entering the fields in shooting light. Instead, they arrive later and later. Hunters are often confounded as to why. The reason, however, is simple: It's the moon! Keep in mind that the moon rises about 50 minutes later each day, and causes deer to instinctively change their movement patterns to later in the day. (This is why my favorite tactic—hunting from 11:00 a.m. to 2:00 p.m.—works so well as the season progresses.)

55 "Harvest moon" is a term associated with the first full moon after the autumnal equinox. White-tailed deer expert Charles Alsheimer, in his book *Hunting Whitetail by the Moon*, refers to this lunar phase as the Pre-Rut Moon. In either case, be advised that this moon phase starts the pre-rut activity when the mature does of every herd in the North and South come into a brief 24- to 48-hour estrous cycle. It can be one of the more productive moon-phase periods to hunt. The other moon-phase cycles that hunters should become more familiar with in order to take more deer include Chase Phase of the Rutting Moon, Post-Rut Moon, and Rutting Moon.

56 One complete lunar cycle takes a new moon to another new-moon phase (this is when the moon is dark), in 29 days, 12 hours, 44 minutes, and 3 seconds.

57 The Rutting Moon accounts for most deer activity. I refer to this phase as the "frenzy period," and it's when bucks are constantly on the move, actively seeking out does in estrus. During this period, bucks will chase any doe they encounter in order to determine if she is in or is close to coming into estrus. This phase typically starts two or three days before the full moon, and ends two or three days after it.

58 A full moon that overlaps the rut accounts for one of the most productive times to be afield. More fully mature white-tails are taken under a rutting full moon than at any other time—including during the midday hours. I have long preached that "off-hour" hunting can be very successful—even more so when the moon is full and the rut is in. A full moon during this period virtually guarantees increased midday activity. When the full moon overlaps the rutting cycle, bucks will be on the prowl throughout the day and night. They can't waste valuable breeding opportunities with does just because it's midday!

PART 12

Scent

No matter what you do to hide your human odor—showering, leaving hunting garments outside overnight, using scent-eliminating clothes or products—you can't get rid of it entirely. The simple precautions that follow will help you reduce your odor as much as possible, thus giving you an edge to see and hopefully take more deer.

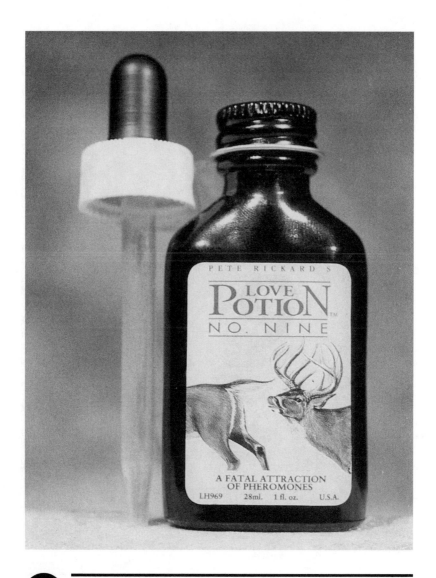

59 If you are using an estrus scent designed to attract bucks, and aren't having much luck, then chances are you're using too much of it. For best results, estrus-type scents should be used sparingly, to imitate the natural amount of pheromones that a doe would naturally deposit when she urinates. Using too much estrus scent will often spook mature bucks, rather than attract them. They know what the real thing smells like, and how strong it should be. Use too much, and they'll know that something is not right.

60 The theory that you can only use food-type scents in areas where that food is present is incorrect. (Many hunters, for example, will tell you that you can only use apple scent in areas that have orchards.) The fact is that deer use their sense of smell to locate danger, find estrous does and other deer, and uncover food sources—especially those edible items that may be out of sight or hidden under leaves. Deer *do not* detect danger from an apple or acorn that they find in an area where that food doesn't occur naturally. To test this theory, wait until after the season, then place a few apples along a deer trail in an area where you're absolutely sure that apples don't grow. The first deer to come down that trail and see or smell the fruit will immediately go to the apples and eat them—not paying any attention at all to the fact that the apples shouldn't be there. For best results when using a food-type attracting scent, use the food scents in areas that the food you're trying to imitate *doesn't* naturally grow.

61 When using a doe estrus scent, don't put it on your clothes or close to your stand. It's more effective to use the scent as a decoy. Instead of placing the scent directly on the bottom of your boot, for example, apply it to a boot pad or rag. When you get to within 40 yards of your stand, remove the pad and hang it from a branch upwind of any deer trails, or bedding or feeding areas. Remember, the scent is meant to attract bucks. If it is too close to you, a buck may be able to see or smell you before he detects the scent.

62 In deer camp, a variety of odors—cooking, tobacco, pets, woodstoves, fireplaces, gas burners—can permeate your hunting clothes. When eating meals (especially breakfast, just before you go hunting) or hanging out in the evening, wear clothes other than the ones you intend to hunt in. By keeping unnatural scents out of your clothes, you'll stand a better chance of remaining undetected by deer once you're in the woods.

PART 13

Decoys

Decoys can range from the traditional store-bought models to unorthodox versions such as hunter scarecrows, fake fruit, and even mounted deer heads and rumps. The use of decoys is only limited by your imagination.

63 Many factors should be considered before you buy or make a decoy, including: gender, weight, portability, visibility, quietness, versatility, practicality of use, natural appearance to deer, and, what has worked best for me in my 35 years of decoying, uniqueness!

64 Not all decoys have to be the standard traditional types of products to work. If you don't want to buy a manufactured decoy, you can easily make one from cardboard or plywood. With a little creativity, some paint, and scent, they can work surprisingly well. Or you can use a mounted buck or doe head (always drape a large blaze-orange cloth over the entire head when walking in and out of the woods when using this tactic). Or you can use cloth or rag decoys, with deer tails or faces imprinted on them. You can also make a human scarecrow (like the kind used during Halloween), and place it so that deer get accustomed to seeing a human form in a certain spot, or position it to intentionally scare deer away from one route and guide them onto another—where you are waiting for them. Or how about using fake fruit such as a plastic apple or ear of corn. Spray apple or corn scent onto the fake fruit, leave it along a known deer trail, and watch the deer come in to check it out.

Finally, the decoy I have had the most success with is a real deer tail. I attach it to a long string, drape the tail over a branch, hide in my stand, then pull on the string, twitching the tail, whenever I suspect that real deer are in the area.

65 Try to match the decoy you're using to the place and time you're hunting. Aggressive-looking decoys, such as a big-antlered dominant buck, don't always work best. While in some instances a large-antlered decoy buck will agitate an aggressive buck into responding, it will also intimidate smaller and sometimes even average-sized bucks, which you may have happily taken, from responding.

Remember that with any type of decoying, calling, or rattling, aggressive tactics usually work against the hunter rather than for him.

66 A wise man once said nothing is more important than location, location, location. Nothing could be more true when it comes to decoying. For decoys to work, deer have to see them. They'll attract deer when set up along the edges of fields, heavily used trails, overgrown meadows, in orchards, and on the edges of swamps. They also have the ability to work in heavy cover. A decoy set up in thick cover can attract deer you didn't even know were there.

67 Here are a few other crucial points when using decoys. Always pay attention to the wind direction. Bucks will often stop and stare at a decoy and then approach it by circling downwind. Try to use decoys whose heads are not staring straight forward. When possible, give a decoy movement by using a brown handkerchief taped to the ear or tail area. In addition to masking your own odor, use a sex or cover scent to encourage deer into responding. Because a buck will always respond to a decoy by walking up and smelling it, wear rubber gloves when setting it up. It also doesn't hurt to occasionally wash your decoy with nonscented soap to remove any foreign odors.

PART 14

Rattling

Let's begin by eliminating the hearsay that rattling only works in Texas. Rattling is a tactic that works anywhere bucks fight, which means virtually everywhere whitetails roam. Of course the more bucks there are in an area, the more competition there is between them for the rights to breed with does. If you're hunting an area with a good to excellent buck-to-doe ratio, rattling will draw in agitated bucks that are willing to throw caution to the wind to get in on the action in a hurry.

68 As with turkey hunting, the setup in rattling is crucial to success. Your stand site should always offer a good view (this doesn't necessarily mean a vast or long view), in whatever cover you choose. But it should give you unobstructed lanes through which you can see and shoot responding bucks. Equally important, it must offer a view of the area downwind of your position. No other single factor will bring you more success. Over the 30 years that I have been rattling, I would estimate that 80 percent of the rattled-up bucks I have taken were downwind of me. For a variety of reasons, almost all bucks respond by putting the wind into their nose. Because of this, staying as scent-free as you possibly can is also a key to success.

A good site also offers saplings to shake and rub, branches to snap, leaves to rustle to simulate the sounds of hooves, and a bare spot in the ground to thump the backs of the antlers.

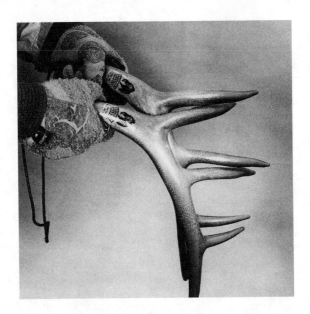

69 Hunters who rattle have long debated the merits of natural versus synthetic antlers. Even though I have rattled with synthetic antlers for 20 years, I have found that both work equally well if you pay attention to a few factors. When using natural antlers, for example, make sure they're fresh, no more than three years old. Don't use natural antlers that are bleached out and dry. The tone they produce will not be natural. If a buck responds, he will do so very cautiously. If you use synthetic antlers, make sure the tone sounds natural. Some do, some don't. Test them outside of the store to get their real sound.

70 Most fights are between bucks from the same herd that have already established their pecking order. So most encounters between combatants will be nothing more than brief pushing and shoving matches. The real down-and-out battles usually occur when a transient buck moves through another buck's territory. The mature resident buck(s) will be quick to forcefully drive him out.

Even these down-and-dirty fights between mature bucks don't start out aggressively, however. Rather, they begin slowly and gradually build to a crescendo. Do the same when you are rattling. Begin by ticking and meshing the antlers together, then slowly build to clashing and banging.

71 Rattling success also depends on you imitating all the other sounds that two bucks inevitably make when fighting, pushing, or shoving one another. This includes the snapping of branches, thumping of hooves, bumping into saplings, grunting, skidding on leaves, wheezing, and, of course, antler meshing. The sequence of sounds that I have had the most success with begins by hitting the antlers together once loud, then gently ticking the antlers together, followed by grinding and meshing the tines slowly while gently rustling leaves and then snapping a small branch or two from a nearby sapling.

PART 15

Calling

While there are about 13 deer vocalizations that biologists have categorized, only 5 help hunters attract deer. They are the snort, grunt, blat, bleat, and, in some instances, the sound made by a very agitated buck—the grunt-snort-wheeze. All work well depending on the conditions.
Most hunters miss opportunities to stop deer, call them closer, or blindly call them in because they either don't know how to use the calls properly, or don't have confidence that they work. We've all been brainwashed to believe that we have to remain absolutely quiet in the woods. No advice could be farther from the truth. Deer deal with noise in their world all the time—especially from other deer. The only noises that will make them nervous are sounds that obviously come from human beings: a human cough or sneeze, voice, a mechanical type of noise from a gun or bow, and so on.

72 It is important to learn how to make each vocalization long before the season begins. Start by watching and listening to deer in fields and along roads from January on. Deer are most vocal in spring and summer, a good time to watch, listen, and then try calling deer. Soon you'll learn not only what calls work—but when, where, why and how to use them. You'll also learn just how loud (or soft) you should call to attract a deer and just how far away a deer has to be to hear your vocalization. By doing so, you'll gain invaluable confidence for using your deer call during the hunting season.

73 When using a grunt, blow it softly. Like rattling and decoying, most times aggressive tactics (calling deeply and loudly) will intimidate lesser bucks from responding to your call. You may even intimidate a buck you may have been willing to shoot. You'll have more success if you sound like a buck that another buck is able to chase off, rather than a buck that will kick his butt!

74 There are four different types of grunts. The *Contact Grunt,* which does and bucks make all year long, is the loudest of the grunts. It is often made by a doe warning off another deer or reprimanding her fawns. It is also made by bucks trying to intimidate other deer. It is an extended, burplike vocalization.

The *Trail Grunt* is a vocalization that a buck makes when he has his nose to the ground and is following the scent of a hot doe. This cadence is a series of very low, almost inaudible clicks and burps.

The *Tending Grunt* is similar to the Trail Grunt and is often confused by hunters. It is slightly louder than the Trail Grunt and is much more guttural in its origin. This is the grunt most hunters can hear from a distance. While it is louder than other grunts, it is not aggressive, but rather runs in a series of long burps.

The *Hot-Doe Grunt* is made by does that are in maximum heat. They are actively searching out bucks by calling to them. It is an extended vocalization of burps, mixed with an extended blat. The doe is basically saying, "I'm here and I'm ready. Where are you?"

75 Other important vocalizations include different cadences (or types) of blats and bleats. A blat is made by a mature deer. There are also five different bleat sounds that fawns and yearlings make. The most important blat is the *Locating Blat*, while the most important bleat is the *Fawn Distress Bleat.*

The *Locating Blat* is made by a doe looking to call her fawn to her side. It is a good call to use when you want to put a doe in the freezer. It's a short but fairly loud sound. Fawns respond to it quickly.

The *Fawn Distress Bleat,* often confused with the blat, is a neonatal vocalization used by fawns that are in peril from a pre-dator or who are being harassed by a buck. Does respond to this call instantly. Sometimes they are followed by their yearling offspring—which could be a buck.

76 One of the most useful sounds a hunter can imitate is the *snort*. There are five cadences of the snort. Each has a different and definite purpose. One is meant to attract, another to stop, a third is used to intentionally scare deer from cover, a fourth sound is to calm spooky deer, while the last is an aggressive call.

The *Alarm Distress Snort* can be one of the most effective deer calls when used properly. It is especially useful when you're hunting alone. I use it to intentionally scare deer from heavy cover. For instance, you can blow the call when walking along ledges to see if a deer will stand up below you. Or blow it when passing a field of standing corn to see if you can make a deer nervous enough to run from the security of the cornfield to other cover. It can also be used to roust deer from gullies in the Rockies or in the high grasslands of states such as Iowa or Kansas. It may also act to drive deer from cover like swamps and thick patches of evergreen trees to hunters waiting on known escape routes.

PART 16

Scrapes

The real fact about hunting over scrapes is that hunters don't kill as many bucks as the magazines would lead you to believe. Taking a buck at a scrape requires time, understanding, and skill. If scrape hunting was as simple as some experts would have us think, we would all be taking trophy bucks each fall. Following is the real "dirt" on scrape hunting.

77 Although some experts say there are only three or four types of scrapes, I believe there are *six* distinct types of scrape classifications. Beginning from pre-rut on, I call them the *Transition, Secondary, Primary, Boundary, Post-Rut,* and *Instinctive Scrapes.* Each refers to a distinctive time, pattern, and locality of the scrape made. Scrapes are excellent indicators of how the rut is developing in your hunting area at any given point and time.

Transition Scrapes are made as a result of photoperiodism—shorter days. As a buck's hormonal levels increase, he begins to act out breeding behaviors. This scrape is small and is usually made in early fall. It is meant to break up the bachelor herds. They are often made midday by bucks that are at this stage and still undisturbed by hunters.

Secondary Scrapes occur as the rut progresses and are usually made at first or last light, or at night. These scrapes are a bit larger than Transition Scrapes. They are made as bucks start to become more aggressive toward each other, usually around the last two weeks of October. You most likely find them in large numbers in areas where they were no scrapes just the day before. Most are left to dry out over the next 48 hours.

Primary Scrapes are much larger (three by three feet and bigger), and are most often made in thick cover and core areas. They are made by mature bucks. Does relate to them visually first, and from their size and scent recognize them as being made by the more physically fit bucks. They are attracted to them, as opposed to the smaller scrapes made by lesser bucks. These scrapes can be made any time of the day or night. They are strategically placed in thick-cover-type areas by bucks who have learned that does frequent these spots. They are made with privacy (security) in mind as well. I like to freshen these types of scrapes with buck urine. When freshening primary scrapes, keep in mind that the buck is often within 100 yards, lying in cover and scent checking his scrape. Action could occur within minutes of placing a competitive buck urine in a primary scrape, as big bucks often respond immediately to this tactic.

Boundary Scrapes are the most recognized by hunters. They are randomly placed, and are generally made in heavily traveled doe social areas, which become frequented by bucks as the rut progress. They most often appear along the edges of overgrown fields, trails, creek bottoms, fencerows, logging roads, and crop fields. Because they are made by bucks wandering home ranges as well as new

areas, and by bucks that have undergone considerable hunting pressure by now, they are often made after dark—and, in some instances, at the crack of dawn.

Post-Rut Scrapes. Older does that are not successfully bred and fawns that never had their first heat cycle during the primary rut can

come into heat at least half a dozen times until they are bred successfully. This occurs well after the primary rut is over, and can be a very active rut phase. Bucks will make new scrapes and refreshen any scrape they come across to attract these hot does. I have seen several bucks on the trail of one doe during this time of year. The bucks are so preoccupied with actually finding the hot doe that they don't spend a lot of time making or standing by these Post-Rut Scrapes.

Instinctive Scrapes. Scrape activity may continue long after breeding activity is over. This behavior is instinctive and will sometimes occur year-round. These scrapes are made randomly by bucks that, without regard to place or time, will simply paw out a scrape. Bucks make them almost as a passing thought. They can be found throughout a buck's range. Hunters locating these scrapes in August are sometimes totally confused by their presence.

78 *Mock Scrapes.* All things considered about scrapes, I don't recommend that hunters spend much time hunting over a majority of the different natural scrapes found in the woods. Instead, I like to make (build) fake (mock) scrapes. Mock scrapes will attract passing bucks via their olfactory senses. The "newcomer's scent" is often quickly checked out by resident bucks looking for the intruder.

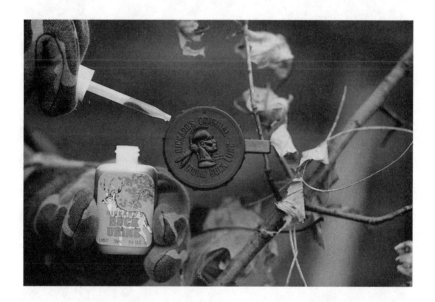

PART 17

Rubs

A rub can tell a hunter a lot about where a buck is bedding and where and what he is feeding on. Rubs play a critical role in a buck's world, especially before and into the breeding season.

79 First establish the general location of feeding and bedding areas in the area you hunt. Then try to find a rub. When you find one (or more), determine what direction the buck was traveling from when he made the rub. If the rub is facing a field, you've discovered the buck's route to his food source. If it's facing known bedding spots, you've found a clue to his general hiding spots and his core area. Because you know that bucks move to feeding areas at dusk, and back to bedding areas at dawn, you'll even know what time of day or evening the buck is moving along that particular trail.

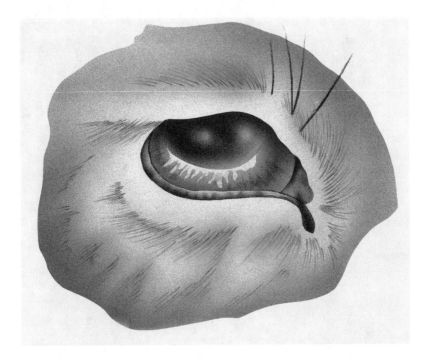

80 Rubs act as visual and olfactory marking posts for bucks, and can attract bucks from long distances. Bucks regularly rub the glands in the corner of their eyes and from their foreheads on rubs to announce to their presence in an area. Other deer can determine exactly which buck made a particular rub, or who the last buck was to freshen it, simply from smelling the rub.

81 Contrary to popular belief, all bucks share rubs. Rubs act as scent-marking posts, meant to communicate important social information to other deer. A rub can tell a deer a lot about the last buck to rub the tree, including his status in the pecking order and his rutting condition. Some biologists believe rubs can even communicate a deer's mood to other deer.

82 Another fallacy about rubs is that small ones are made by small bucks and large ones by big-antlered bucks. Over the past two decades of videotaping my television program, *Woods n'*

Waters, I have taped small 10- to 14-inch-wide bucks, forkhorns, and even spikes making rubs on very large trees—some with sizable diameters. I have seen them rubbing big cedar trees bare of bark. I have also videotaped mature racked bucks, with 8 points and more and 18-inch-plus spreads, rubbing small saplings. The real tip here is not to place any credence in the adage about big bucks and big rubs. To really know just how big the buck is that made a rub, you have to actually see him making it.

83 One of the most effective hunting tactics I have used over the years is to create mock rubs. Because they act as both visual and scent-marking posts for other bucks, mock rubs can be incredibly effective. Take a knife or handsaw and vigorously rub the bark off a tree—being careful not to cut too deeply into the tree and injure it. Start 4 to 6 inches from the ground and rub up about 18 to 20 inches high. Don't make it too big, as you'll intimidate more bucks than you'll attract. Next, take forehead scent from a buck a friend may have taken or a commercially made one and place a drop or two on the tree. Get ready. The first buck that comes up the path and sees the rub will have no choice but to inspect it. It's simply a matter of instinctive behavior.

PART 18

Wind Direction

Overlook the wind, and you'll be in for a long and fruitless deer season. When you think of wind, remember this phrase: Bust a buck's nose, and you'll bust the buck.

84 Wind is the key to successful deer hunting. The hunter who doesn't pay strict attention to wind direction each and every time he goes afield will never be consistently successful. Keeping the wind in your favor will help you see and take more deer, especially more mature bucks.

85 Meteorologists define wind as air in horizontal motion relative to the surface of the earth. Wind is better identified as ascending or descending currents—and not really wind at all. Each type (current, thermal convection, prevailing breeze) has its own nuances, and each carries human odor differently. For instance: A thermal current is caused by the heating and cooling of the earth's surface. Human scent will ride a thermal current around a deer stand and inevitably cause problems.

86 White-tailed deer, especially bucks, survive predominantly through their primary sense of smell. Almost every deer hunter has witnessed a buck questioning what he sees. He may doubt a message sent to his brain from his eyes or ears, but he will never second-guess a message sent to his brain from his sense of smell—*Never*. Deer use air currents to help detect their relative safety or danger when they are traveling or bedded down.

87 Pay attention to any difference you may detect in the wind, as this can indicate whether the wind is going to change direction, or become cooler, warmer, drier, or moister than the air you are currently encountering. A sudden change in wind direction could also indicate that there may be a change in weather coming. Perhaps a high or low pressure system is about to move north or south of the area you're hunting. If you monitor changes in wind, you will be able to better plan your current day afield or your next day's hunt.

PART 19

Walkie-Talkie Tips

When using walkie-talkies, remember that they should be used as hunting tools and not as telephones. Too many hunters use their radios to have idle conversations while on deer stands. Most hunters don't realize that by doing so, there is a good chance deer will hear the voices and avoid the area entirely. And make no mistake, deer can hear the talking even if both hunters are whispering. Also, talking with a friend on a two-way radio is like talking on a cell phone while driving a car. You're just not able to pay full attention to what you're supposed to be doing at the time—hunting. It doesn't take a deer long to slip by undetected while you're on the radio asking your buddy, "Did you see anything?" If you're on the radio instead of paying attention to the hunt, the answer inevitably will be no.

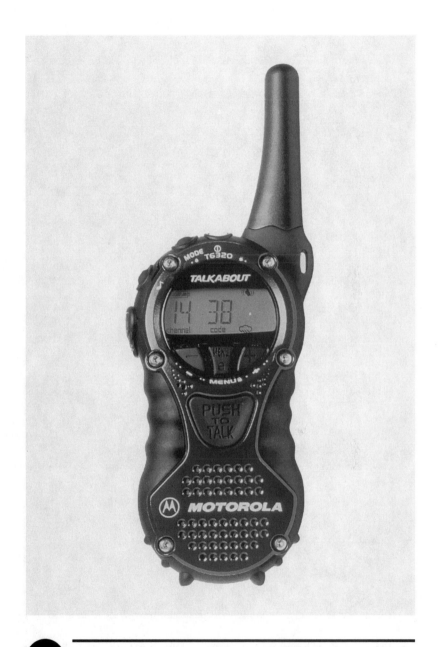

88 When using a radio, keep the volume and squelch controls at their lowest levels. When you must talk with a hunting companion, just click the "talk" button three times to indicate that you need to talk with him. This sound is much lower and move

unobtrusive than constant whispers emanating from your hunting coat or backpack. Only talk on the radio when you must tell your partner something important. Keep all conversations short.

89 To eliminate unnecessary movements, use a clip-on speaker and earphones so you don't have to keep bringing the unit up and down to your mouth. Deer can pick up such movement from quite a distance away. Combine that with the noise they hear from the static and clicking and your voice, and you've just tipped the odds more in the deer's favor.

PART 20

Food Plots

Over the past 10 years, hunters have learned the value of planting food plots. These islands of nutrition not only help to improve the deer's overall health and antler growth, but can also serve as a dependable way to attract deer to your stand.

90 When planting any food plot, especially clover, till the soil and plan to broadcast (plant or spread) the seed when the forecast calls for at least an entire day of steady drizzle. A few days of light rain would be best. This will help the seed to take hold, root quickly, and then begin to grow.

Make sure the seed you are using is a quality seed that is germinated and inoculated. By doing so, you will drastically eliminate any chance that your crop will have a high concentration of weeds in the seed.

91 Food plots don't always have to be planted. In fact, you can use natural vegetation to attract deer. By simply pruning plants such as berry bushes, wild apple trees, grapevines, persimmons, and the like, you can help the plants produce more fruit. To enhance the production further, you should also fertilize a pruned bush or tree at least twice a year—in early spring (May) and again in early fall (October). I especially like to fertilize white oak trees. I select one mature oak in different areas that I hunt, and twice a year I use Jobe's Fertilizer Spikes to help the tree produce bigger, sweeter, and more acorns. In some instance, I have been fertilizing the same oak tree for years. Such trees always produce a healthy crop of acorns, even when the surrounding oak trees aren't. It's a way of attracting deer, bears, and turkeys to the same location each fall. It doesn't take wildlife long to learn that a particular oak is a food source they can depend on—and only you know what tree it is. This food plot/decoy tactic works even on public ground.

PART 21

Tips on Oaks

*A deer's number one choice of foods is acorns,
especially from white oak trees. Acorns provide
deer with a source of high protein in their diet.
Identifying an oak can be a daunting task for
some hunters. If you really want to increase the
number of deer you see, hunt the oaks. The easiest
way to identify the different oak trees is by their
leaves. A hunter who knows his oaks will soon
be dressing out a good buck.*

92 *White Oak* is a common oak tree and can be found in Canada and most parts east of the Mississippi. It is most common in New England and the Northeast states. Its leaf features noncorresponding rounded points.

Red Oak: The red oak is most common in the North, and can be found in Michigan, Wisconsin, Illinois, throughout New England and part of the Northeast, and Canada. Its leaf features corresponding points that are jagged.

Live Oak can be found in most coastal plains states, and is common in Texas, Florida, Alabama, Mississippi and Oklahoma. Its acorn is small and oblong, and its leaf is round with a tough skin.

Water Oak can be found in the coastal plains and adjacent areas, and is common in New Jersey, Florida, Texas, Missouri, Oklahoma, and Mississippi. Its thin leaf is oblong, featuring three rounded points.

PART 22

Field-Judging Antlers

One of the most complicated aspects of deer hunting can be field-judging (scoring) a set of antlers before shooting a buck. This has to be done quickly, and somewhat accurately. The entire process is totally dependent on the buck. If he sticks around long enough for the hunter to estimate his rack, the tactic works. If not, deciding whether to shoot or not can only be done if you understand there may be "ground shrinkage" after the buck is down. To accomplish this task quickly and easily, hunters have to keep just a few guidelines in mind.

93 The most critical factor for a typical set of antlers to score high is symmetry. The more "even" both sides are with one another, the higher the antlers will measure. Therefore, when trying to quickly determine if a buck you are looking at will score high, make sure the tines on one side of the rack are as close to being equal to the other side as possible. Any difference will be a deduction. Also remember that the more tines the rack has, the higher it will score. A typical 8-pointer has less chance of making the B&C books than a typical 10-pointer does.

94 The next important step in evaluating a rack is to try to determine the inside width or spread of the buck's antlers. You can get a good idea of the spread by looking at the buck's ears. Typically, the average buck's ears, when held out to side of his head in the alert position, measure between 16 and 18 inches tip to tip.

95 Another critical factor in scoring antlers is the overall length of each main beam. The longer, the better, provided both are approximately the same length. Again, the difference will be a deduction.

96 Now look at the overall mass (thickness throughout the set of antlers). The thicker the antlers from the base up, the higher they will ultimately score. Generally, pencil-thin racks do not score well.

97 The key to field-judging is to check all of the important elements as quickly as possible. So long as the buck doesn't walk off in the middle of the process, you can do this task in less than a minute once you become experienced at it. And therein lies the reality of field-judging a buck's antlers on the hoof. Most bucks will not give you the time to score their racks as I have just described unless they are slowly moving through an area or feeding— and they don't feel threatened. If you're thinking about becoming a trophy hunter, practice by estimating the scores of whitetail mounts. By estimating the size of every set of mounted antlers you see, you will become better at judging what a set of antlers will score. In time you will be able to field-judge a buck's antlers in seconds rather than minutes—thus helping you quickly decide whether to take a particular buck or not.

PART 23

How Old Is That Buck?

If you're a serious trophy hunter or just want to know more about the bucks you take, learn how to judge the age of a buck in the field before you shoot him. It will help you to learn how to manage the deer in your area, so that bucks develop bigger antlers from one year to the next. It will also allow more does to pass his genes on to future generations. Knowing how old a buck is will also tell you about the quality of the nutrition he is getting from the land, whether or not he possesses superior genetics, if he should be culled from the herd, and, most important, if he should be passed up for a season or two in order for him to mature and grow a much larger rack. For instance, killing a buck whose antlers have a 17-inch inside spread, some mass, and good beam and tine length, only to find out he was a yearling to 2½-year-old buck, could be a big mistake. With a little time, a buck like this could have been a real trophy-class whitetail.

98 When talking about how old a deer is, the age is most often expressed in years plus one-half (1½, 2½, 3½, and so on). The reason for this is that deer are born in early summer, and by the time they grow their first set of antlers, they are usually one year and six months old.

147

99 Three basic elements allow bucks to grow large antlers: genetics, nutrition, and age. Both the doe and the buck contribute *equally* to the genetics of their offspring. If both partners carry the DNA to produce big antlers, then their offspring buck will have the potential to grow large antlers as well.

If all the contributing factors that help develop a buck's antlers are "normal" throughout his first 4½ years of life, and he has not incurred any serious injury or health problems, he will develop his biggest set of antlers when he is 5½ to 6½ years of age. Much depends on the amount and quality of forage he ingests in that particular year.

100 When trying to age a deer on the hoof, keep in mind that a 1½-year-old yearling buck looks more like a doe with antlers than a buck. He has a small head, a lean face and neck, and long legs. He is slender looking from shoulder to flank, and his rump may appear higher than his shoulders. Finally, he acts submissively to other bucks and does.

Most 2½-year-old bucks look evenly built from neck to rump. Their stomachs and backs don't sag. They have thick briskets, their necks are heavier than those of the younger bucks that usually accompany them, and the skin on their face and neck is tight.

The most difficult age to determine with accuracy is the 3½-year-old buck. He has almost the identical characteristics of a 2½-year-old buck, but his hindquarters are rounder, and his neck and brisket are much thicker and more pronounced than those of younger bucks.

A 4½-year-old buck has now hit middle age, and looks like an adult. His overall body is thicker, his belly looks fuller, his hindquarters are more muscled, and, most obvious, his legs look shorter compared to the rest of his body.

At 5½ years old, a buck begins to lose his overall youthful looks. He starts to look older. While his neck is much larger than that of other bucks, his stomach and back sag somewhat, his rump looks smaller than his shoulders, and the skin around the face is looser. The most obvious trait is that his eyes lose their roundness, and bucks begin to look as if they are always squinting. (Note: Gray hair may not always be a reliable way of judging an old buck. Many young bucks have inherited a trait for grayish hair.)

At 6½ years and older, all bucks begin to look alike. They are in the twilight of their years. Their faces and necks are loose and flabby, their backs curve deeply, and they have big potbellies. Their noses are puglike, showing the wear and tear of years of fighting with other bucks. Most noticeable for me is the way bucks of this age walk. Their joints are stiff and they walk in a slow, deliberate gait. Finally, their antlers may begin to grow erratically from here on in, and, in some instances, become gnarly and smaller than when they were in their prime.

PART 24

Aging Deer Teeth

*The only reliable way to determine the exact
age of a deer is by checking and counting its teeth.*

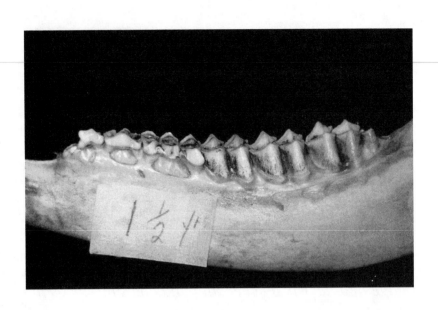

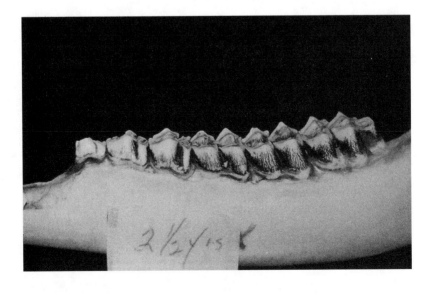

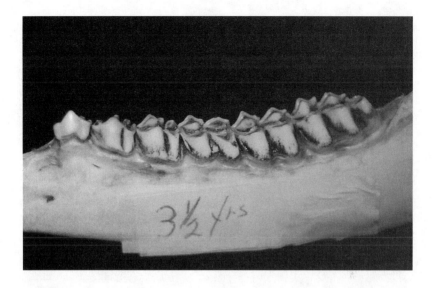

101 Once you have taken a deer and want to determine its age, first count the teeth. There are 32 in a mature deer. Take one of those teeth and mail it to the deer specialist at your state's fish and game department. He or she will cut the tooth and count the rings, as foresters do with trees, to get a precise aging. While other factors such as swayed backs, hanging stomachs, puffy eyes, and puglike noses can suggest a buck's age, only the teeth will reveal for certain how old he really is.

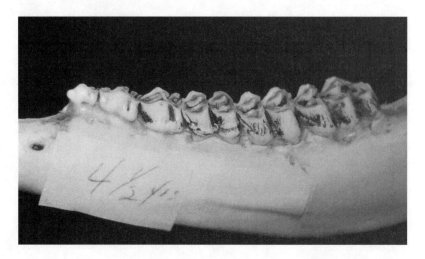